Ancient Innovations

The Technology of Ancient China

Jason Greenling

Cavendish Square
New York

Published in 2017 by Cavendish Square Publishing, LLC
243 5th Avenue, Suite 136, New York, NY 10016

First Edition

Library of Congress Cataloging-in-Publication Data

Names: Greenling, Jason, author.
Title: The technology of ancient China / Jason Greenling.
Description: New York : Cavendish Square Publishing, [2017] |
Series: Ancient innovations | Includes bibliographical references and index.
Identifiers: LCCN 2016021838 | ISBN 9781502622358 (library bound) | ISBN 9781502622365 (ebook)
Subjects: LCSH: Technology--China--History--Juvenile literature. |
Science--China--History--Juvenile literature. |
China--Civilization--Juvenile literature. | China--History--Han dynasty,
202 B.C.-220 A.D.--Juvenile literature.
Classification: LCC T27.C5 G76 2017 | DDC 609.51--dc23
LC record available at https://lccn.loc.gov/2016021838

Editorial Director: David McNamara
Editor: Kristen Susienka
Copy Editor: Nathan Heidelberger
Associate Art Director: Amy Greenan
Designer: Joseph Macri
Production Coordinator: Karol Szymczuk
Photo Research: J8 Media

The photos in this book are used by permission and through the courtesy of: Cover Jan Koldijk/Moment Open/Getty Images; p. 4, 49 Pictures from History/Bridgeman Images; p. 6 Izf/Shutterstock.com; p. 7 World History Archive/Alamy Stock Photo; p. 9 Yves Andre/Moment/Getty Images; p. 10 File:Potassium nitrate.jpg/Walkerma/Wikimedia Commons; p. 11 Marilyn Barbone/Alamy Stock Photo; p. 12 Keren Su/Corbis Documentary/Getty Images; p. 14 Barney Burstein/Corbis Historical/Getty Images; p. 17 ilbusca/iStockphoto.com; p. 18 Elena Sherengovskaya/Shutterstock.com; p. 20 Philip and Elizabeth De Bay/Historical Picture Archive/Corbis/Getty Images; p. 21 Xing Guangli/Xinhua/Alamy Stock Photo; p. 22 Wilson's Vision/Shutterstock.com; p. 26 Ariana Lindquist/Bloomberg/Getty Images; p. 28 RUKSUTAKARN/Shutterstock.com; p. 30 feiyuezhangjie/Shutterstock.com; p. 33 lapas77/Shutterstock.com; p. 36 Zhang Peng/LightRocket/Getty Images; p. 38 IMAGEMORE Co, Ltd./Getty Images; p. 40 Science & Society Picture Library/Getty Images; p. 43 China Tourism Press/The Image Bank/Getty Images; p. 44 wissanu01/iStock/Thinkstock; p. 46 Visuals Unlimited/Getty Images; p. 51 British Library Board. All Rights Reserved/Bridgeman Images.

Printed in the United States of America

Contents

Chinese rulers like Yu the Great were said to have abilities such as taming rivers and lakes.

Chapter One

The Wise Men's Gifts

In world history, China's past spans thousands of years. In fact, it is the world's oldest continuous civilization. China's past directly connects to its present. It has ancient legends that tell of **culture heroes** and wise leaders bringing gifts to the first Chinese people. These gifts transformed the country and the people living in China. What were they? Technologies. These gifts helped the Chinese build great structures and run a powerful civilization that continues today.

The Gifts of the Heroes and Wise Men

Using only native bamboo and hemp, one culture hero taught the Chinese how to weave fishnets and trap animals. Another hero invented agriculture. He taught people how to till the land with plows and plant crops such as **millet** and rice. He also showed people how to use various plants as medicine and to brew tea, a plant native to China.

The legends relate that after the time of the culture heroes, wise kings and their ministers brought gifts of technology to the Chinese. The Yellow Emperor fought a great military battle in a thick blanket of fog. Although he couldn't see anything, he won his battle by using technology in the form of a compass to plan the movement of his troops on the battlefield. His spectacular victory unified northern China.

The ancient Chinese established many innovations, including farming methods and irrigation.

One of the Yellow Emperor's ministers invented writing by observing the footprints of birds and other animals. He taught people to keep records by carving words into turtle shells and bones. Each graphic character carried the meaning of a separate word. Today, the Chinese still write with characters instead of combining the twenty-six letters of the alphabet the way Westerners do. Chinese schoolchildren need to memorize thousands of characters. But each character is part of a word picture linking today's students with the ancient world of their ancestors.

The Yellow Emperor's wife taught women how to raise silkworms, moth larvae native to China. She taught the women how to feed the silkworms mulberry leaves until they spun cocoons around themselves made of silk strands. She then instructed women in the technology of unwinding the silk strands from the cocoons, spinning the strands into silk threads, and building looms to weave the silk threads into silk cloth. Chinese silk was so prized in the ancient world that it was traded as far as Rome.

A portrait of the First Emperor, who unified China under the Qin dynasty in 221 BCE

The Emperor That United a Country

In 221 BCE, the first unified Chinese empire was formed when seven warring states were united by a conqueror from the state of Qin, who declared himself China's First Emperor. He immediately set forth proclamations controlling his empire's technology in order to unify his newly enlarged kingdom. He standardized weights and measures across the empire. He declared a set width for the axles of chariots so that a man could travel on China's grooved roads from one end of the empire to the other without stopping to change carriages. He standardized written Chinese characters so that people who spoke different **dialects** could still understand one another's writing. Even today, when Chinese people watch movies, many depend on subtitles, the spoken words of the movie written on the bottom of the screen. This is because while the Chinese speak varying dialects, they all write words using exactly the same characters.

Emperor Yu the Great, the founder of the Xia **dynasty**, China's first dynasty (2205–1818 BCE), tamed the waters of the Yellow River in northern China. The people needed the waters of the Yellow River to farm, but they often suffered from floods that destroyed their crops and drowned many people. The clever emperor built a vast and complex system of dikes and drainage areas. A Chinese proverb says, "The Yellow River brings one hundred sorrows, but there are riches on its bend." Yu's gift of engineering technology allowed the Chinese to settle and farm, developing the area around the Yellow River.

The gifts of these heroes and wise kings allowed the ancient Chinese to build an empire. They are still used today by over one billion people in twenty-first-century China, the world's most populous country and an emerging **superpower**. These ancient inventions and many more have been confirmed by **archaeologists** working in China. In the future, as the Chinese build up their country's highways, railroads, and cities, they certainly will continue to uncover vast

The Yellow River

numbers of ancient sites where their ancestors lived. Such excavations allow archaeologists and other scientists to paint a more accurate picture of the amazing technologies invented by the ancient Chinese.

Chinese Technologies Today

Isolated from other great ancient civilizations by mountains and deserts, China developed distinct technologies that are uniquely Chinese. These continue to be a feature of Chinese civilization to this day. Many of these ancient technologies depend upon native plants, animals, and minerals found in the vast and varied landscape of China itself. Lacquer, made from the sap of the lacquer tree, a tree native to China, gave the ancient Chinese the world's first plastic. Mulberry trees and hemp were used to produce the world's first paper. Native silkworms gave the ancient Chinese silk, the world's strongest natural fiber. Bamboo, a species of huge, hollow grass, was used for pipelines in irrigation and mining. Natural deposits of **saltpeter** led to the development of gunpowder.

Saltpeter

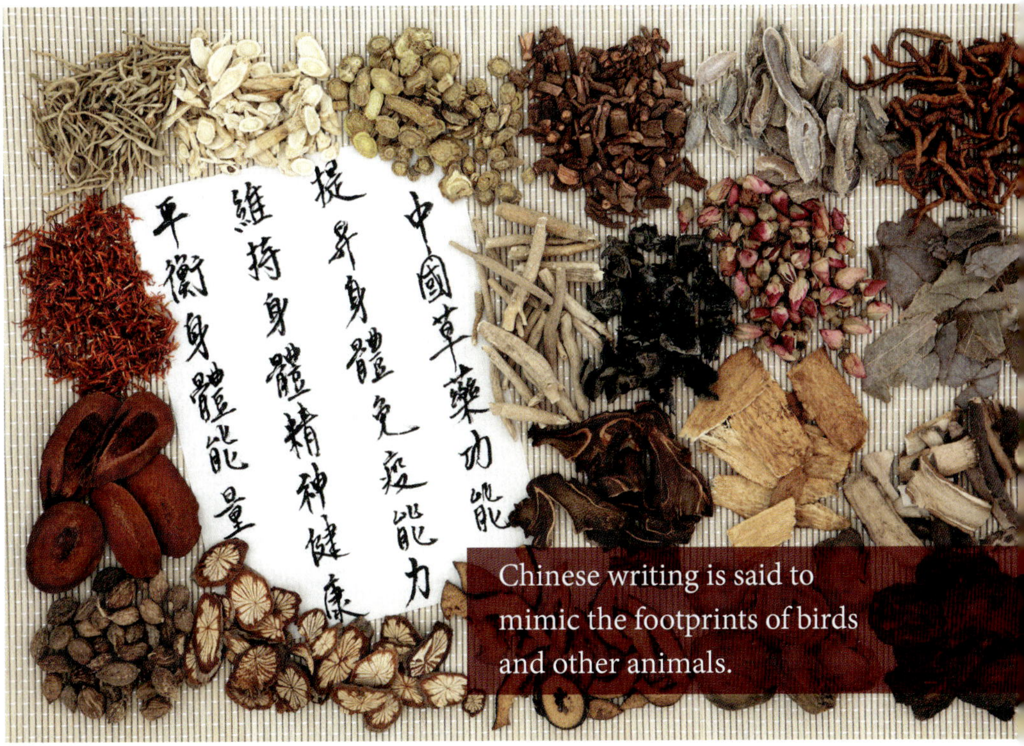

Chinese writing is said to mimic the footprints of birds and other animals.

Chinese scientists continue to develop technologies based upon native Chinese materials. These are combined with the most up-to-date techniques to produce a uniquely Chinese technology. The resulting products are used in fields from modern medicine and space exploration to manufacturing and construction. Chinese doctors and scientists are experimenting with native Chinese plants to find drugs to combat epidemics and other deadly diseases.

As more technologies continue to be discovered, modified, and applied to modern industries such as medicine, agriculture, and construction, all have their roots in ancient Chinese technologies. This testifies to China's versatility as a nation of invention. It remains an important source of innovation in the modern world.

People plant wheat on a loess plateau.

Chapter Two

Technologies That United a Nation

The history of how China evolved into a unified, technologically advanced nation is vast and full of triumphs and downfalls. Many technologies developed quickly and became popular with society, continuing into today's modern techniques.

A Country Unites

In 221 BCE, the first unified Chinese empire was formed when seven warring states were united by a conqueror from the state of Qin. He declared himself China's First Emperor, the Son of Heaven, and established the Qin dynasty (221–206 BCE). The First Emperor unified the country through warfare, but he would build his empire through controlling its technology. He immediately set forth proclamations controlling his empire's technology. As one of his first acts, he set a uniform width for the axles of chariots and carriages and started constructing a vast network of standardized roads.

The ancient roads of northern China were not built on the surface of the ground but into the earth of China itself. The north of China is covered by a thin, fine soil called **loess** that blows across the region from the Gobi Desert. Building roads on top of such soil is inefficient, as they would quickly be buried by blown loess. Instead, ancient

Chinese built their roads by carving out two grooves in the soil that would act like the gauges of a railroad for the wheels of chariots. The fine soil was compressed by pounding it with cobblestone pestles. The standardized axle widths and roads meant that people could now travel throughout the empire on horse-drawn carriages and chariots without having to change vehicles. Chariots were used to transport supplies and imperial administrators.

The Han Dynasty

The Qin emperor was a brilliant but harsh ruler, and his dynasty could not last. It came to an end shortly after the death of the First Emperor, and the Han dynasty was established (206 BCE–220 CE). The Han based their rule on the idea that the emperor had to take care of his people. This was called the **Mandate of Heaven**. To make sure that the people were protected and had enough food, the Han emperors turned to technology. During the Han dynasty, technological advances in transportation allowed the empire to settle into a single political power with a central administration.

This painting shows a royal entourage moving through the Chinese mountains during the Han dynasty.

As the Han empire grew, horses were crucial for maintaining contact and control throughout the immense and diverse country. It was during this era that the chariot emerged as the main means of empire unification. Men and goods alike needed to reach the farthest limits of the Han territory. During the Qin era, horses had pulled chariots with a harnessing system based on the one used to control the power of oxen. This system employed a yoke with straps around the neck of the ox. This arrangement had serious drawbacks. The throat strap pressed directly on the animal's windpipe, so the horse began to suffocate quickly.

The Chinese of the Han dynasty sought a technological solution that would allow them to use the great strength of the chest of the horse for pulling. During the Han period, the Chinese invented a more efficient harnessing system. One theory about this breakthrough in transportation technology is that it was based upon the human harness system used for hauling boats upstream on China's rivers and canals. Effective pulling could be achieved only when men pulled with the power of their chests. The Han Chinese added a breast strap to the harness so that the horse's powerful shoulders were surrounded. Next they fitted the horse with a collar in the form of an artificial hump, like that of an ox. Now the load moved by the horse was pulled by the power of the horse's chest and collarbone. Another factor that certainly influenced the development of the collar harness came from the camels that trekked the **Silk Roads** of northern China. The camel caravans of the Silk Roads were composed of Bactrian camels, the two-humped camels whose twin humps had been fitted with collars on which baggage was tied. It was a logical step to adapt this technology to horses.

During the Han dynasty, improvements were made to the Qin road system. An elaborate arrangement of three-lane imperial highways that crisscrossed the Chinese empire was constructed. The central lane was reserved for the emperor himself as well as members of the royal court. The outer two lanes were used by court officials. The highways had a series of approved rest stops to be used by officials. Each rest stop was stocked with horses so that imperial affairs of state were not held up.

During the Han dynasty, the emperors organized the army to include a cavalry of soldiers mounted on horseback. At the beginning of the dynasty, the soldiers rode with simple saddles, their legs just hanging over the sides of the horse without stirrups for their feet. They were not efficient fighters. They were forced to grip the manes of their mounts with one hand and press their legs tightly to the horse's flank in order to avoid slipping off. Also, it was difficult to mount a horse while carrying weapons.

By the end of the Han dynasty, a variety of saddles with stirrups, saddle pads, and saddlecloths were found throughout the empire, and a military saddle supporting the hips and upper legs had emerged. The Han army, mounted on horseback, could quickly travel to the farthest reaches of the empire. They were a fierce and efficient cavalry that protected the borders of the empire and actually expanded Chinese territory.

Building Ships

The Chinese also used the rivers and tributaries that crisscrossed China for moving men and goods. They developed the technology to make their boats and ships efficient for water transportation. The Chinese quickly realized that they could capture the power of the wind to propel their ships. The earliest Chinese sails were made not of canvas as in the West, but of bamboo **battens** with woven matting stretched between them. The sails could be adapted to wind conditions by being folded up or let down, much in the way that a set of venetian blinds is raised or lowered. The battens held the sails taut, making them more efficient than canvas sails. By staggering the masts on the ship, instead of having one single row along the center of the deck, the Chinese ensured that one sail could not block the wind from reaching the sail behind it.

Introducing the Stirrup

The invention of the stirrup solved the problem of both mounting a horse and defending oneself on horseback. Early stirrups were simply a flat oval with a long handle made from iron or bronze. Other versions would be introduced and popularized over time. This gear led directly to the use of mounted cavalry as a military force in China. During the Han period, the throne established a standing army that could quickly be deployed to any spot on the map requiring defensive action. With an effective and mobile cavalry, China could defend its northern borders against the restless nomadic people and ensure the safety of its agricultural heartland.

This illustration shows a Chinese rider using stirrups to stay on a horse.

The Chinese also adopted a rudder to help them steer their ships in the currents of the great rivers of China. A rudder is a flat piece of wood attached to the stern, or back, of a ship, so that the vessel can be turned, causing the front of the ship to turn in the same direction. A slung rudder is a rudder that can be raised or lowered using rope tackle. This meant that the rudder could be raised when a boat entered shallow water, protecting it from being snapped off on a shallow river bottom.

This reconstruction of an ancient Chinese ship sails the waters today.

During the Han dynasty, in the second century CE, the Chinese constructed their ship **hulls** on the bulkhead principle. A bulkhead is a solid wall separating compartments belowdecks. This meant that if a leak or accident occurred in one section of the ship, it could be sealed off from the other compartments. Thus the ship would remain afloat until repairs could be made when the vessel reached a safe harbor.

These watertight compartments could also work so that selected compartments of the ship could be flooded. In this way, water could be taken onto the ship to act as **ballast**. Adding water would make the ship heavier and lower to the waterline so that it could sail more effectively in calm, deep rivers. Water could be released from the compartments to raise the craft when shooting rapids in a river and to avoid rocks. This technology also worked from a commercial point of view. For example, Chinese boats transporting fish brought their catch to shore still swimming in one or several compartments—fresh fish at the market!

This technological advancement in shipbuilding was probably invented when shipbuilders observed the characteristics of bamboo, a plant native to China. Bamboo is a very large grass species. It has membranes that cut across its stem horizontally so that the hollow stem is divided into a series of separate sealed compartments. By observing this native plant and applying the same principles into bulkhead ship construction, the Chinese were able to modify shipbuilding to ensure the safety of passengers and cargo.

Building Bridges

The Chinese also developed technology to help bridge the country's rivers so that people and goods could be transported across them. The earliest form of bridges in China likely began when ancient Chinese used a bow and arrow to shoot rope from one riverbank to the opposite one. The rope was anchored on each side, and men would cross over the water by going hand over hand, holding the rope to pull themselves across. This was difficult and dangerous. Only one person at a time could cross the river. A man had to use all his strength to pull himself along the rope, so he could not carry much of anything heavy, like a weapon or goods.

In order to protect men's hands from rope burn as they pulled themselves across the river, the Chinese began to wrap their hands with leather or cloth. Then the ancient Chinese again turned to bamboo, the abundant native plant, in their search for improved methods of bridge construction. They realized that they could thread a rope through bamboo, a plant that is hollow in the middle. This use of bamboo meant that a person could slide along the rope with less effort, pulling himself across a river without fear of burning his hands on the rope. Over time the Chinese used this flexible piece of bamboo as a railing when they added a cradle of ropes suspended from the bamboo tube to walk on. Eventually they devised a way to add a woven walkway of matting that could be added to the rope cradle.

This painting shows a bamboo aqueduct. Bamboo was an important building material in ancient China.

With this addition, a man could walk upright across the river while carrying goods.

The suspension bridge, a flat roadway suspended from cables, was invented in China during the first century CE. Again, the Chinese turned to bamboo in their construction technology. Cables were made by using plaited strips of the strong outer layers of bamboo wrapped around a center made from the core of the bamboo. This combination of bamboo materials and construction techniques ensured that the greater the tension on the cables, the more tightly these outer strips of bamboo gripped the inner bamboo core. This idea was a great technological advance, since it meant that the inner strands would break before the outer strands. In this way, the safety of the traveler was assured, and men and goods crisscrossed rivers from one end of the empire to the other.

Today, bamboo continues to be a key element of construction in China. Chinese engineers have found that lightweight and flexible bamboo is the most effective material for constructing scaffolding during the building of modern skyscrapers in booming cities like Shanghai and Beijing. The building process draws upon native Chinese resources, and its roots can be traced back to the technologies of ancient China.

Tall Trains

A bullet train travels on the West Loop.

The People's Republic of China continues to build on its ancient technologies with cutting-edge transportation engineering. In 2006, the Tibetan Railway opened a rail line that had the same **altitude** as some commuter flights in the United States. In order to build a railway line here, Chinese engineers had to devise special technology to cope with the harsh environment, the thin air, and the shifting, fragile ground of the Tibetan Plateau.

They continued the railway evolution in 2015, when China announced another rail feat, the opening of a 215-mile (346-kilometer) West Loop high-speed rail line. This track circles the popular Hainan Island. Passengers can visit all kinds of terrain on this journey. To date, it is the world's first high-speed railway that circles an island. From these experiences, China continues to be a leader in innovation and advises other countries on their methods of high-speed transportation.

A farmer works a terraced field in Guilin, China.

Chapter Three

Agricultural Technology in China

Agriculture has always been an important industry in China. Farming and cultivation techniques have been developed over the centuries and continue today. In modern times, the practical application of Chinese farming technology is based upon labor-intensive work that has been practiced for millennia. Crops are planted and harvested primarily using human muscle power. This means that Chinese farming depends upon one of China's greatest resources: the enormous population of the country. This resource is available because, over the centuries, China's farming know-how has allowed the Chinese population to increase to such large numbers. There has almost always been enough food. This impressive agricultural success began with ancient China's technology.

Important Tools

The ancient Chinese grew millet in northern China and rice in the south. In order to prepare soil for planting the crops, farmers first need to break up the surface of the earth by cutting **furrows** into the soil. A plowshare is used to dig into the earth and turn over the soil. Examples of ancient Chinese stone plowshares date from 4000 BCE. These stone plowshares were heavy and not very efficient for breaking up the soil.

Tin and copper are two metal resources found in China. Around 2000 BCE, the Chinese discovered that they could melt tin and copper and combine them to make a new metal. The combination of two or more metals is called an **alloy**. Copper and tin were combined to make the alloy called bronze. Bronze is harder and more durable than either tin or copper. Bronze resists corrosion and wear, to a certain extent. The Chinese cast tools and weapons from bronze using clay molds into which the hot molten metal was poured.

Advances in the science and technology of metals, called **metallurgy**, led to the manufacture of iron in ancient China. The Chinese learned to mine iron ore and extract the metal from the ore. The earliest iron was brittle and unsuitable for farm tools. Rocky soil caused frequent breakage of these early iron tools. By the third century BCE, however, the Chinese had made improvements in their cast-iron technology, upgrading the strength of the metal and quickly adapting it for farming technology.

A new kind of plowshare called a *kuan* took advantage of this improvement in metallurgy. The kuan plowshare had an iron central ridge with a sharp point. From this point, two wings sloped to throw the soil off to either side of the blade. This design reduced friction on the plow, so it moved more easily through the soil. Farmers could also regulate the plowing depth by adjusting the distance between the plow blade and the beam or framework of the plow held by the farmer. This control allowed farmers to fix the capability of the plow to deal with the characteristics of the soil, different weather, and various crops. This technological improvement allowed the Chinese to bring new lands under cultivation.

Along with the cast-iron plow, ancient Chinese agricultural technology included the use of a small iron seed drill. The seed drill is a device that allows the farmer to place seeds into furrows in the prepared soil. A seed drill is pulled along the furrows made by the plowshare so that seeds are dropped directly into the furrows for growth. Before developing this mechanism, the ancient Chinese had used the broadcast method for planting seeds, where a farmer simply scatters seeds by hand onto the plowed earth. Using the broadcast method, a farmer might count on only about half of the valuable seeds actually ending up in the prepared furrows. The other half of the seeds are blown away by the wind or eaten by birds.

At about the same time the seed drill was invented, a new type of long-handled iron hoe was introduced. This hoe had a curved handle and was called the swan-neck hoe. The new hoe was designed to allow farmers to work the soil around plants without damaging them. Hoeing enables farmers to clear their fields of weeds, break up hard soil so that plants can emerge, and draw up earth around growing plants to protect them. Hoeing is most efficient when crops are planted in the straight rows or furrows made by the plow. Since all of the seeds are planted at about the same depth by the seed drill, all the plants will be about the same height and easier to hoe.

The new iron hoe had several blades so that farmers could change them throughout the growing season. This technology meant that a farmer could use a single tool to meet different needs at the different stages of crop growth and cultivation. A farmer would use one blade to hoe around small seedlings and clear away weeds. He would bank up the earth around these small plants with a different blade. Yet another blade would be used to break up the soil around mature plants.

Farmers of the Past

After the crop was harvested, edible grain kernels had to be removed from the straw or stalk. This was done in a method called **threshing**. In ancient China, threshing was done by beating the crops with heavy stones to separate the grain from the straw. Then the seed coverings, or chaff, was separated from edible kernels in a process called **winnowing**. The winnowing was accomplished by using the power of the wind. In this process, the farmers used large woven baskets to toss the grain into the air. The wind blew away the lighter chaff, and the heavier grain was caught again in the basket. This method was both time consuming and

Chinese farmers thresh rice stalks in 2011.

inefficient. A farmer and his family had to toss the grain into the air many times to rid the seeds of all the inedible chaff. As the wind blew away the dusty chaff, some grain was lost.

A more efficient method of winnowing technology was developed with the invention of the rotary winnowing fan during the second century BCE. Models of winnowing fans have been found in tombs dating to the Han dynasty (206 BCE–220 CE). This agricultural technology used a strong current of wind produced by a crank-operated fan mounted on one side of a **hopper** or box. The grain was fed into the hopper through a funnel on top. When the crank was turned, the blades of the fan produced a strong gust of air. This wind from the fan blew the chaff away and out through a vent in the side of the hopper. The heavier grain fell to the bottom of the hopper, where it was collected. This type of fan was portable and could be used by several farming families or rented out. More grain could be winnowed by this method than by tossing the grain in winnowing baskets. Less grain was lost in this process because it was collected in the hopper as it was processed.

During the first century BCE, the Chinese invented a cart with a wheel to help farmers transport farming supplies and harvests. This cart, later called a wooden ox or a gliding horse, is familiar to us today as the wheelbarrow. The Chinese-style wheelbarrow, with a single large wheel, could be pulled by long handles in front or pushed by such shafts from behind. With the introduction of this technology, a single man with a wheelbarrow could now move hundreds of pounds in a single trip. Using a wheelbarrow could cut in half the number of workers needed for transporting crops. Just as sails were used to capture the wind on boats, the Chinese sometimes affixed small sails to the bodies of their wheelbarrows in order to harness wind power, enabling farmers to more effectively transport crops and supplies.

Early Irrigation

In order to ensure irrigation of farmlands and a supply of drinking water, the movement of water by means of a pump was invented during the Han dynasty, in the first century CE. The **endless chain pump** is a device that can still be seen today in rural China where man power is still used instead of electricity or gasoline. The pump is a circulating chain of square pallets. These pallets are flat wooden blades that can haul water from lower to higher levels. The power for the chain pump comes in the form of human leg muscles on pedals that push the pallets down into the water again and again. Leaning against a short fence, Chinese farmers literally walk miles on the pedals, using the muscle power of their legs to lift water to the fields. The pedals turn a large cogwheel that pulls the chain of square wooden pallets, and the water spills into an irrigation ditch on a higher level. Two people working this machine can irrigate hundreds of plots of farmland.

Silk

In addition to grain, every Chinese household had to contribute bolts of woven silk to the government as part of their taxes. Silk was valuable as it is stronger than any plant fiber known, and it keeps the wearer warm in the winter and cool in the summer.

Standard-sized bolts of silk were used as money from the Han dynasty onward. Silk was used to pay government officials' salaries, to clothe the army, and in imperial rituals and diplomacy. The Chinese have continuously made silk from at least 3000 BCE. The raising of silkworms, the harvesting of their cocoons, and the spinning of silk thread is called **sericulture**. Sericulture depended upon the technological expertise of Chinese women and the use of an animal and a plant both native to China—the silkworm and the mulberry tree.

A woman weaves silk on a loom.

Silk production begins with the hatching of tiny silkworms in the spring. These larvae are deposited on woven bamboo trays and fed on the leaves of mulberry trees. Their light gray skin feels dry and papery. After about five weeks of care and feeding, the worms begin to spin their cocoons around themselves from a strand of a sticky white substance that comes from their bodies. This is the substance that turns into silk thread. A single continuous strand of silk may run for between 660 and 1,000 yards (600 and 900 meters). This silk strand is carefully unwound from the cocoon onto wooden bobbins. To make up the thread, several silk strands are twisted together by means of a spinning wheel. The silk thread is then woven into cloth on a loom by crossing horizontal threads with vertical threads in an over-and-under way, using a variety of patterns. It takes from 2,500 to 3,000 cocoons to make 1 yard (about 1 m) of silk fabric. The older worms, or pupae, in some cocoons are allowed to mature and become the moths that will lay more silkworm larvae.

During the Han dynasty, silk weaving reached new heights. Han women developed weaving techniques producing complex and beautiful patterns in the silk fabric. Their silks were traded along the Silk Road as far away as Rome. The Romans referred to China as "Serica," meaning "Land of Silk." During this time, the Chinese saying "Men sow and women weave" came to mean an empire that was peaceful, productive, and well ordered.

Agriculture Today

China's influence in agriculture can still be seen today. For example, the country is the world's largest producer and consumer of rice. In many countries in Asia, people obtain the overwhelming part of their needed calorics by cating rice. The government of China has established institutes to help tackle global famine by constantly improving farming methods and developing new types of rice for farmers worldwide. Other farming methods, such as silk farming, continue to hold significance. Despite more artificial and quicker ways of producing materials such as silk, China remains a leader in silk production around the world.

The Great Wall of China took many years and many hands to build.

Technologies That Built China

During the civilization's existence, the Chinese became known for their many innovative construction methods. They built cities, dams, and walls to make better their livelihoods. These are some of the technologies that truly built China.

Loess and Pounded Earth

Winds from the Gobi Desert blow east across the plains of northern China. As the wind rushes across the rugged landscape, it carries a fine yellow soil. Some of this soil, called loess, is found in the water of the Yellow River, turning it a muddy yellow color. Over the centuries, the loess has settled on the plains to form deposits to depths of 110 to 330 yards (100 to 300 m). The ancient Chinese used the loess of the northern plains as a construction material, creating solid building foundations and towering walls that surrounded and protected their cities. They developed a technology called **pounded earth**, or rammed earth—*hang tu* in Chinese—to take advantage of this unique building material.

Pounded earth construction compacts the fine loess soil into a durable building material. The first step in this technology is to construct wooden frames by lashing together the trunks of small trees. Soil is dug from the earth with spades and placed in woven baskets. The baskets of soil are carried to the work site, and the loose soil is dumped into the frame. It is then pounded with cobblestones. These are large stones made smooth and round by river currents. The cobblestones are lifted by means of a wooden lever and brought down on the soil again and again. The pounding reduces the bulky loose soil into thinner and tightly packed layers of soil. These compact layers are built up again and again using the same process. Since each layer of compacted soil is only a few inches in thickness, the process must be repeated many times in order to build up a structure.

In ancient China, these compacted layers of soil were so tightly packed that in many places they still survive today. They have a hardness similar to that of concrete. Impressions from the cobblestone pounders are sometimes still visible on the outer surfaces of the top layers excavated by archaeologists.

A form of pounded earth technology is still used in building construction by the people living in the countryside of northern China. This technology is popular today because buildings constructed of this natural building material keep people warm in the winter and cool in the summer. The loess building material is readily available, and it's free!

Archaeologists studying ancient Chinese sites that used pounded earth technology have examined this modern process in order to better understand ancient technology. They used their observations as the basis for calculating the number of men and the amount of time needed in the construction of the wall surrounding the ancient city of Zhengzhou built in northern China during the second millennium BCE. The wall used 1.14 million cubic yards (870,000 cubic m) of pounded earth. They estimate that it took thousands of workers nearly ten years of labor to build this ancient city wall.

A Great Wall

The oldest sections of China's Great Wall were constructed using pounded earth technology. The Great Wall was begun in the third century BCE. At this time, seven warring states in China built walls of pounded earth to defend themselves against invaders as well as to launch attacks against their enemies. When King Zheng of the state of Qin defeated the other warring states, he became the First Emperor of China. The First Emperor joined a series of these pounded earth walls together to form the Great Wall. He joined the walls built by his defeated rivals into a continuous rampart about 1,500 miles (2,400 kilometers) long. For this reason, the Chinese name for the Great Wall actually translates as "the Long Wall." It remains the longest man-made structure in the world.

The First Emperor commanded his general, Meng Tian, to take charge of this ambitious endeavor to construct a defensive line across the northern frontier of his empire. He wanted to protect his kingdom from the nomadic people to the north. Meng Tian **conscripted** legions of laborers, including convicts, soldiers, and women, for this project. The work was a combination of repairing and connecting the defensive walls built by the states that had fought against and lost to the First Emperor. While building the wall, many people died, and rather than take time to lay them to rest, many were buried within the walls themselves. Archaeologists have excavated sections of the Great Wall in order to study these ancient men and women who sacrificed their lives to the monumental technological project.

The Great Wall is the best-known achievement of the Qin dynasty (221–206 BCE). Most of what we call the Great Wall today, however, was built during the later Ming dynasty (1368–1644 CE). The survival of the oldest sections of the Great Wall into the modern era, nonetheless, attests to the technological skill of those ancient builders. The Chinese word for "city" comes from the word ***cheng***, or "wall," because the ancient Chinese typically surrounded their cities with towering walls of pounded earth.

Qin Warriors

The terra-cotta warriors are an impressive relic of the Qin dynasty.

In addition to the Great Wall, another feat tackled during the Qin dynasty was the building of the emperor's **mausoleum**, or death chamber, and its treasures inside. The First Emperor took to the throne at the age of thirteen. Soon after, work on his mausoleum began; however, it was never finished. As the Qin empire collapsed in the third century BCE, a rebel army raided the pits surrounding the First Emperor's tomb. The rebels destroyed many of its treasures and set fire to wooden support beams used in the construction of the pits. In 1974, the tomb was discovered. When archaeologists looked inside, they were shocked to find the remains of over eight thousand life-size **terra-cotta** warriors and horses. The warriors were arranged in battle formation according to rank, and each had its own facial expression. It is thought each soldier would accompany the emperor on his journey to the afterlife. After many years, Chinese archaeologists have painstakingly restored each fixture as a tribute to the ancient unknown artisans and their amazing technology.

Ceramics

After unifying the seven warring states, the First Emperor built his capital city in Xianyang in northern China along the banks of the Wei River, a tributary of the Yellow River. Over the centuries, the shifting course of the Wei obliterated most of this ancient Qin capital. Archaeologists carried out a geological survey in 2010, however, that revealed a city laid out along a grid system of intersecting avenues and streets, thought to be the remains of Emperor Zheng's Xianyang. Archaeologists believe that the primary palace of the new capital was a multilevel structure with pounded earth foundations. The main building was flanked with symmetrical wings.

The new empire got a capital that was grand, luxurious, and built using innovative ceramic technology. The buildings of Xianyang were decorated with brightly colored ceramic tiles. Ceramic pipes were used to construct a central heating system. These pipes carried heated air through the buildings to keep the First Emperor and his court warm and comfortable during the long, cold winters. Plumbing for the buildings was also constructed from ceramic pipes. The bathrooms had ceramic pipes to carry away wastewater and empty it into the Wei River.

Ceramic was also used to create the terra-cotta soldiers in the First Emperor's mausoleum. Each figure was painted in brilliant colors and equipped with a real weapon made of bronze, including swords, halberds, and crossbows. Chariots were equipped with terra-cotta horses wearing bronze tack.

All these projects required considerable skill in ceramic technology, starting with the building of **kilns**. These are the ovens used to bake or "fire" clay into pottery. The Chinese had a unique method of construction for these kilns. Unlike kilns in the West that are actually separate structures of brick, the Chinese built their kilns into the sides of hills. This construction technique uses the simple premise that heat rises. In order to take advantage of this principle and achieve higher temperatures while using less fuel, the Chinese

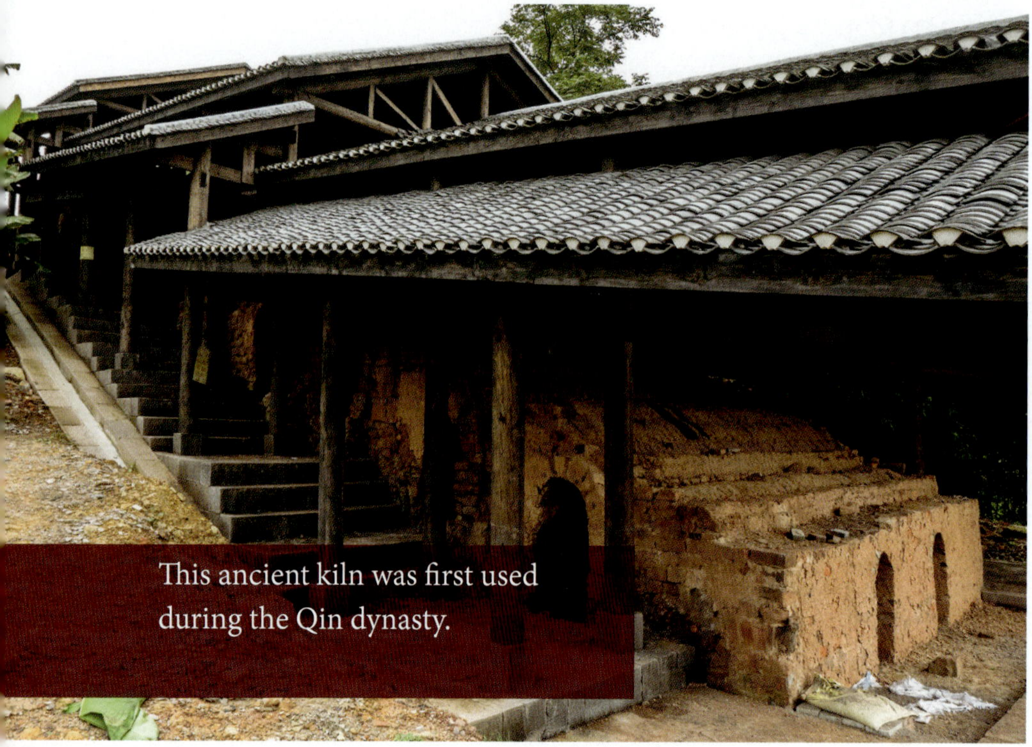

This ancient kiln was first used during the Qin dynasty.

built their kilns into the landscape of China itself by making tunnels in the hillside that followed the natural contours of the land. The kilns ran zigzag, with several openings, or mouths, on the side of the hills that could be used for regulating the temperature and firing conditions. The Chinese dubbed these kilns "dragon kilns" because they coiled their way along the natural contours of the earth like a writhing dragon.

All these massive construction projects involved innovative technology as well as a huge expenditure of materials and manpower. Some archaeologists estimate that fully one in ten people labored on construction projects during the First Emperor's reign. The cost in human effort and suffering was enormous and provoked the people to rebel. A large-scale uprising put an end to the Qin empire in 206 BCE after only fifteen years.

Today, China is the world's most populated country, with more than 1.3 billion people. Modern engineers are constantly inventing new ways to accommodate a growing country. As more and more superhighways, airports, and railways are built, more of China's ancient past is unearthed. It is truly a marvel to see such accomplishments from centuries ago.

Old Technology Used in a New Way

The 2008 Beijing Summer Olympics gave the Chinese the chance to present the face of modern China to the world. The Beijing National Stadium was the main Olympic site for track and field events as well as the opening ceremony of the Olympics. The stadium is the world's largest steel structure and can hold eighty thousand spectators. Known as the Bird's Nest due to its shape and the unique lattice of steel on its exterior, the stadium symbolizes a cradle, holding the hopes of mankind for the future.

Chinese artist Ai Weiwei was the consultant for the stadium's Swiss architects. Together they studied ancient Chinese ceramic technology for inspiration. One result of this search is the unique cooling and heating technology used in the stadium. Rainwater is collected and purified, then pumped into pipes under the stadium's playing surface. There it is heated in the winter and cooled in the summer, similar to the ceramic pipes used for heating and drainage at the First Emperor's capital at Xianyang.

This image shows a Chinese goddess. Some inventions were said to be divinely inspired.

Chapter Five

Technologies That Ruled China

In ancient China, there were many factors that led to new inventions and technologies. Sometimes these factors involved messages or signs from the divine.

Mandate of Heaven

The ancient Chinese believed that Heaven sent signs to show approval or disapproval of the emperor's rule. When his rule was kind and just, Heaven would send good weather and abundant harvests. When the emperor failed to act correctly, Heaven would show its displeasure. These natural phenomena were part of the Mandate of Heaven.

When Heaven disapproved of the emperor's rule, terrifying comets would light up the night sky. During the day, eclipses would block the light of the sun, frightening the people. Droughts, floods, and earthquakes would destroy crops and homes. When these events occurred, it was the emperor's duty to come to the aid of his people and reform his behavior. He would perform religious rites beseeching Heaven to spare his people from suffering. He helped the people by sending them aid in the form of food, soldiers, or workers to confront their suffering.

A Scientist of the Past

A reproduction of Zhang's seismograph

Zhang Heng is one of the few names to which we can attribute contributions to Chinese science and technology. He is perhaps most well known for his invention of a **seismograph**, which detected earthquakes in the region. Zhang's books, *Bird's-Eye Map* and *Discourse on New Calculations*, are known to us only by name, having been lost centuries ago. This was likely because special works were stored in secret archives. During Zhang's time, possession of superior maps was crucial to calculating the time it would take to move men and goods. Therefore, accurate maps were the key to ancient Chinese military and political success. For this reason, early maps were not copied and were very often destroyed. The top-secret information on maps was just too critical for the emperor to risk their falling into the wrong hands. Chinese archaeologists are hoping that future excavations of Han-period tombs will bring to light lost works by this luminous Chinese scientist. Their discovery will make his work better understood and appreciated.

Earthquake Technology

The emperors used men at their courts to help them predict, pinpoint, and interpret these signs from Heaven. For the ancient Chinese, distinction was made between the regular and predictable side of nature versus irregular and unpredictable events. Unpredictable events were considered warnings. These communications were left for learned men to interpret. One such man was Zhang Heng, who served the Han emperors during the second century CE.

Zhang Heng called upon technology to help foretell these events and uphold the Mandate of Heaven. First, he drew upon new technology to map the heavens. Zhang did this to help set a yearly calendar, a pivotal innovation. This calendar was used to establish the time frame for rituals that the emperor performed on behalf of his people. Zhang's calendar was also used for setting the schedule for festivals celebrated throughout the empire.

Zhang Heng used China's advanced metal technology to devise instruments to map the sky. Under his supervision, metal rings divided into degrees were joined together, forming a skeleton around sighting tubes through which one could observe particular stars. The sighting tube was moved until a star was found, and then the number of degrees was calculated. In this way, a logical and precise star map was drawn. Zhang Heng added waterpower to make the instrument rotate and thus predict the movement of the stars over time. Because the North Star and the stars around it were visible all year long, Zhang used these as the focus of his heavenly observations. These included the wheeling around the North Star by constellations such as the Big Dipper. The handle of the Big Dipper pointing south during the summer and north in the winter marked off the twelve months by which the inquisitive ancient Chinese calculated a year of 365.25 days!

Zhang Heng also invented an earthquake detector, a seismograph, for the Han emperor. Zhang's invention consisted of a large bronze vessel with a domed lid about 6 feet (2 m) in diameter. On the perimeter of the vessel were eight dragon heads holding bronze balls in their mouths. Directly beneath the dragons' mouths were eight bronze toads with tilted heads and large open mouths. A ball falling from a dragon's mouth into the mouth of a toad signaled that an earthquake had occurred in the kingdom. The earthquake tremor caused the device to release a ball on the side of the seismograph farthest away from the earthquake's epicenter. This notified the emperor of the site of the disaster so that he could send help. The emperor needed to know exactly where to send extra military forces and food relief, so pinpointing the afflicted area was important. Since the empire collected taxes in the form of grain, the emperor also needed to know if these shipments would be interrupted. He could also order grain from the imperial granaries to be supplied to the people in need. Scientists have made a replica of Zhang Heng's seismograph from its description in written records. To date, though, they have been unable to understand exactly how Zhang Heng's original machine worked. During the long centuries of Chinese history, secrets behind the technology were lost.

China today continues to search for improved technology in order to predict earthquakes and to minimize harm from these terrible occurrences. In 2008, China's Sichuan Province was devastated by a horrific earthquake. Tremendous loss of life occurred due to the collapse of school buildings in which children were trapped. Officials blamed the deaths on school construction using concrete that was not reinforced with steel. In 2010, an earthquake in western China killed more than six hundred people and injured thousands. In 2015, another strong earthquake occurred, measuring 6.5 on the **Richter scale**, in the Xinjiang region, killing four and injuring many others. Chinese engineers are searching for improved construction techniques so that these tragedies can never occur in the future. They are experimenting with flexible building materials that can bend with movements of the earth while still supporting walls, as well as construction techniques that will reinforce the vulnerable areas around doors and windows that often collapse during earthquakes.

The engineers are also testing a plan that includes cameras and a GPS system in vulnerable areas. The scheme, like Zhang Heng's secret maps, will allow rescue efforts to reach affected areas more quickly in the event of an earthquake.

Sometimes, inventions resulting from natural disasters and cosmic happenings had remarkable success. The ancient Chinese, although rooted in the past, developed many successful techniques and innovations that have shocked, intrigued, and puzzled modern engineers and historians.

A Map's Lines

A portrait of Zhang Heng

Zhang Heng also applied the grid system we call **longitude and latitude** to maps of the world. In this system, intersecting horizontal and vertical lines are drawn on an image of the mapped territory. By numbering these lines, a person can pinpoint a location on the map. In 116 CE, Zhang Heng presented the emperor with a map of China using grids. The official history of the Han dynasty states that Zhang "cast a network of coordinates about Heaven and Earth and reckoned on the basis of it." This technology allowed Zhang to calculate distances in an accurate and scientific fashion. This was important for determining the time it would take for the emperor's commands to reach the farthest corners of China. It was crucial during an emergency when the emperor needed to estimate the time it would take for soldiers and supplies to reach a specific point on the map. This mapping technology helped the emperor uphold the Mandate of Heaven by quickly coming to the aid of his people.

Fireworks displays first dazzled ancient China's skies.

Chapter Six

World-Changing Technologies

Throughout its long history, there are four key inventions that changed ancient China and brought it into a modern era. They are: the compass, gunpowder, paper, and printing. These early inventions, while begun in China, did not realize their full potential there. Rather, their inventions expanded to other reaches of the world. Regardless, the entire world was changed by these innovations from ancient China.

Telling Direction

Chinese traditionally attribute the invention of the compass, a device for determining direction, to the legendary Yellow Emperor. Chinese myth recounts that the Yellow Emperor used the compass in a great battle. Because the battle was fought in a thick, blinding fog, the Yellow Emperor was able to use a compass to deploy his troops. The use of this technology assured his victory in the fight.

Historians trace the earliest Chinese use of the compass back to the fourth century BCE, a time before the First Emperor ruled China called the Warring States Period. Those early Chinese compasses consisted of a ladle, or dipper, made of magnetic **lodestone**, a naturally occurring magnet composed of iron ore. The compass consisted of a polished square bronze plate with a rotating lodestone

A lodestone

ladle placed in the center of a circle within a square plate. The square plate representing Earth had geographical directions inscribed on it, and the circular center symbolized Heaven. Within this symbolic map of the universe, the lodestone ladle stood for the Big Dipper (Great Bear) constellation. The compass worked because the bowl of the magnetic lodestone ladle naturally rotated toward the north. When this happened, the handle of the ladle pointed to the south.

The ancient Chinese used this early compass mostly for the magical divination practices associated with **geomancy**. The art of geomancy seeks to discover the interactions between the universe and man, and to apply this knowledge to the management of the environment.

Geomancy is often called *feng shui*, a Chinese term that translates as "wind-water." The ancient Chinese considered where a structure, city, or grave was located crucial for its success. They believed in breaths and currents of energy circulating throughout the universe. These currents are called *qi*. The aim of feng shui is to site structures harmoniously with these celestial currents. In ancient China, the

Reasons for Gunpowder

The Chinese didn't invent gunpowder because they sought a better way to kill people. Instead, the Chinese discovered gunpowder while seeking the elixir of immortality, a magical potion they believed would enable people to live forever. Early Chinese alchemists were convinced that they could combine saltpeter and other elements into a medicine that would increase vigor and longevity. Others were seeking to combine various base metals to obtain gold.

movement of the lodestone compass by a skilled geomancer was used to detect these forces. People would build their houses in auspicious locations to catch friendly forces, bringing good fortune into the home. Conversely, certain movements of the lodestone compass indicated harmful forces that were to be avoided. Feng shui is dismissed by many Chinese as folk religion. It is still a popular practice in China today, however, especially with those in the business community, who seek to increase their fortunes by using it.

By the seventh or eighth century CE, the lodestone ladle was replaced by a needle made out of iron. The needle was magnetized by rubbing it with a lodestone. This development allowed the compasses to be much more accurate, for the needle was thinner and more precise than the lodestone ladle pointer. The Chinese also found that suspending the needle by a single strand of silk thread attached to the center of the needle by a small dab of wax gave a still more accurate reading than placing the needle directly on the board.

By around the year 1000, Chinese were using magnetic needle compasses for navigation. There are many references to Chinese sailors depending upon these compasses in overcast weather when navigation by the stars or land detection was impossible. Ship captains could determine in which direction to steer their vessels by using compasses. They no longer had to keep close to the shore for land sightings and could be more confident when sailing in overcast or stormy conditions.

Historians believe that this awesome Chinese technological invention reached Europeans and Arabs through nautical contact with China in the thirteenth century. Prior to acquiring the compass from Chinese mariners, European ships hugged the coastline of the continent in their voyages, meaning that ship captains could navigate their course only by land sightings during the day and by the stars at night. Free of these constraints, European ships were sent by their kings in search of new lands to conquer. The compass allowed pioneering seafarers from England, Holland, Portugal, and Spain to leave the shores of Europe and venture across the Atlantic Ocean to unknown new lands.

Chinese Gunpowder

Fireworks existed in China from at least 200 BCE, when pieces of bamboo were thrown into fire, where the heat caused the wood to split with a long popping noise. By the seventh century CE, the Chinese had learned that by combining three native ingredients—saltpeter, sulfur, and charcoal—they could produce controlled explosions.

Saltpeter is the common name for potassium nitrate. (Its Latin name means "salt of the rock.") Natural deposits of this chemical are found only in hot climates. Saltpeter can actually burn on its own. So the more saltpeter added to a mix, the more flammable it becomes. Sulfur was obtained by roasting iron pyrites (also known as fool's gold) in furnaces. The resulting vapor would form crystals when cooled and solidified. Sulfur was used to lower the ignition temperature. The third ingredient, charcoal, was readily available and plentiful. It added carbon to the chemical mix so that the ignition could be sustained.

By the year 919, the Chinese had begun to apply gunpowder in warfare. The first use of gunpowder as a weapon was as a long-burning fuse in a flamethrower. This device sprayed enemies with burning

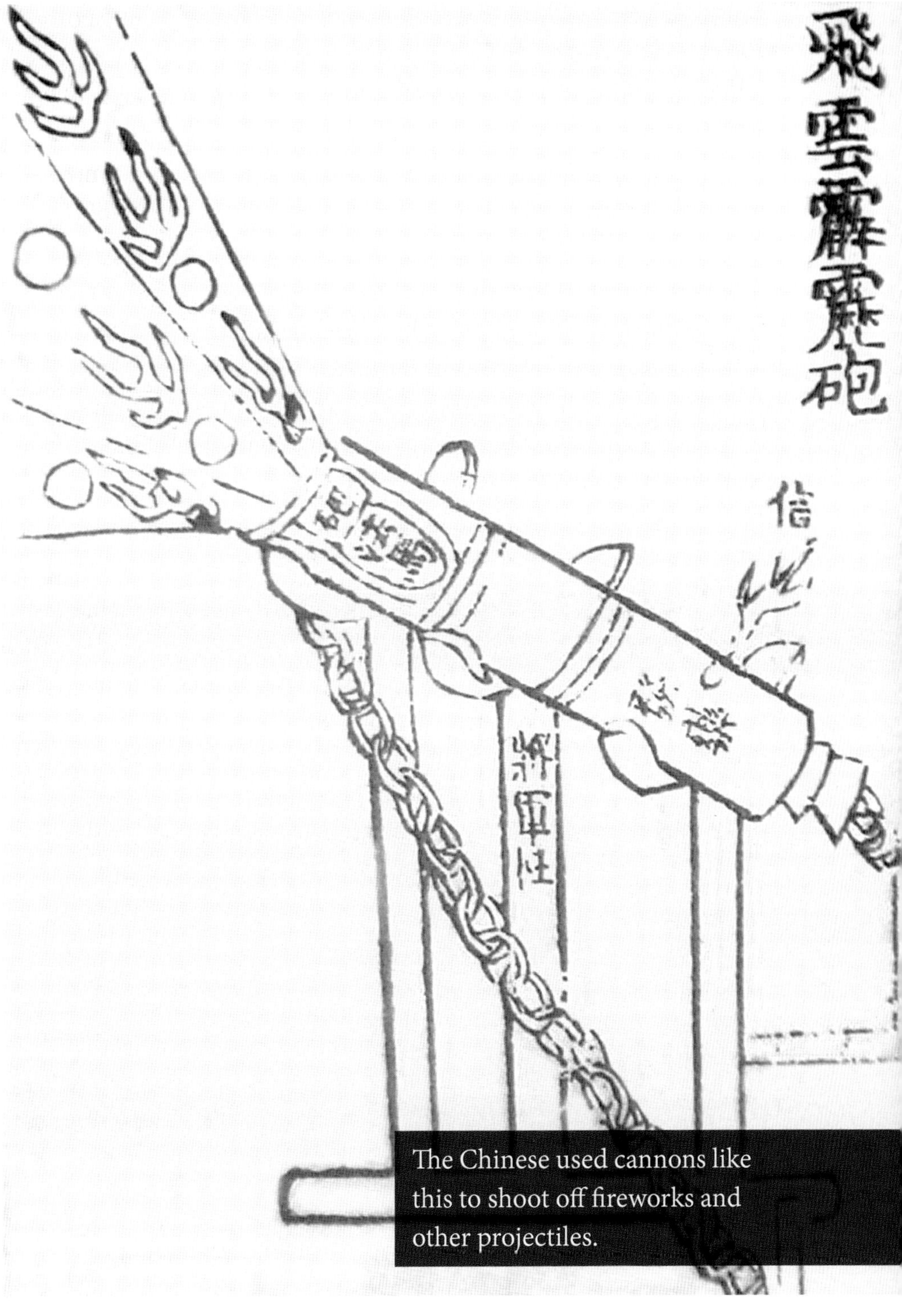

The Chinese used cannons like this to shoot off fireworks and other projectiles.

gasoline or kerosene, which the Chinese knew how to manufacture. As the liquid was ejected from a pump, gunpowder in the fuse ignited the volatile liquid and sprayed a sheet of flame onto the enemy. By the year 1044, the flamethrower was standard issue to Chinese troops.

When the proportion of saltpeter in the gunpowder mixture is increased, true detonation is achieved. The Chinese quickly developed technology for barrel guns and cannons. By the thirteenth century, gunpowder came to the attention of the West, which enthusiastically embraced it. This was an age of tumultuous warfare among the countries of Europe, which constantly launched attacks against each other, as well as organized the Crusades to the Holy Land. The Chinese invention was quickly seen as advantageous, and advances in technological warfare were quickly added to the base of Chinese technology.

Lighting Up the Sky

It was a logical step for the Chinese to apply the new technology of gunpowder to fireworks. By adding elements to these controlled explosions, bright lights could be pitched into the sky, creating dazzling spectacles. Fireworks displays were used at court entertainments during great public festivities such as the celebration of the Lunar New Year.

The technology of fireworks is called pyrotechnics. These pyrotechnic displays included favorite night sky images the Chinese called fire trees, flame flowers, and peach blossoms. Lunar New Year celebrations to this day always include fireworks. The popular belief is that the explosions chase away all the evil spirits that might torment households. It was in the form of festive fireworks that Chinese gunpowder first came to the attention of the West.

An illustration of the papermaking process

Papermaking

The Chinese credit the invention of modern papermaking to Cai Lun (Ts'ai Lun), a man who lived in second-century-CE China during the Han dynasty. Cai Lun made a pulp by chopping up tree bark, hemp, old silk rags, and fishing nets, and then adding water to make a thick soup. He dipped a woven mat into the substance and placed it in the sun to dry out. When this was done, he simply peeled off the dry sheet from the mat. This product was thick, coarse, and uneven in texture—but it was paper.

Earlier forms of paper had been seen as useful for proper hygiene. There is a text from the year 93 BCE in which an imperial guard recommends that a prince wipe his nose with a piece of paper—the world's first Kleenex. Paper was also made available in bathrooms as toilet paper. The crude early paper was also used for clothing, and there are records of people using paper as protective clothing against the wind and as a lining for shoes. Beds were surrounded by paper curtains to keep people warm in the winter and by mosquito nets of thick paper in the summer to shield them from the discomfort of bites and exposure to disease.

It was to be a while before the Chinese discovered the potential of paper for writing. Through technological improvements, the early crude paper was made stronger and smoother by the addition of starch and gypsum, a mineral often used to make plaster, to the paper pulp. Paper eventually was made waterproof and more beautiful by coating it with gelatin obtained from lichens, and by staining and polishing it. This technology made paper suitable for writing. The Chinese quickly grasped the advantage of replacing expensive silk with paper as the main vehicle for writing and painting.

China's Early Printing

The invention of printing in China was a revolutionary technological achievement in the seventh century CE. The craft of printing arose in China some seven hundred years before its appearance in Europe. This was possible due to the earlier inventions of paper and ink.

Printing allowed for books to be produced more quickly than by copying each page by hand. Thus multiple copies of books became cheaper and available to more people than ever before. The ideas in printed books spread rapidly and allowed the Chinese from one end of the empire to the other to share the same ideas, learn the same history, ponder the same philosophical questions, and read the same plays and poetry. Printed words became a main building block for a shared culture, defining the Chinese as a distinct people and setting them apart from their neighbors. Printing became the front door to education and advancement for anybody who learned to read and write. Books, such as this one you are reading now, became commonplace and an essential tool for living in the modern world.

China's Legacy

Today, China's influence on new technologies and the rest of the world is building. The country is a leader in business, the economy, and manufacturing. In recent years, China and the United States have formed closer ties and have worked together in new technological ventures. China's early accomplishments have made it a capable and admirable civilization, one that endured and survived decades of difficult times.

China has emerged in the twenty-first century as a viable superpower exerting influence on the modern age. Looking back, the ancient Chinese established themselves first in areas of transportation, agriculture, architecture, and science. In modern times, they have continued to influence the world. By working together and sharing resources and ideas, the technology of the future is certain to make the world a better, happier, and safer place.

China's Technologies Expand

The Chinese call their country "The Middle Kingdom" and traditionally view it as the center of the world. It is certainly true that China has received and transmitted technology to and from the West and the East. Central Asia, to the west of China, is the entrance to the Middle East. These lands formed the main trade routes on which camel caravans carried men, goods, and ideas between China and her neighbors. The ideas of many Muslim scientists reached China through these trade routes, and Chinese inventions were transmitted to the West. International traders, as well as Christians returning home from the Crusades in the Holy Land, helped spread Chinese inventions through Europe. These inventions changed the course of history during the great European age of exploration. The compass and gunpowder made possible the conquest of new lands in the New World, while paper and printing helped Europeans administer their new territories.

Chronology

The mists of time Wise kings and emperors bring technology to the ancient Chinese, including weaving of fishnets, agriculture, medicine, tea drinking, writing, and silk weaving. Emperor Yu controls the waters of the Yellow River.

3000 BCE First silk used in China.

2205–1818 BCE The Xia dynasty is established in northern China.

thirteenth century BCE Pounded earth building technology is developed.

sixth century BCE Stone plowshares used in farming.

fourth century BCE Called the Warring States Period. Efficient horse harness is invented. The first lodestone compass is devised.

third century BCE The first contour transport canal is constructed. Iron plowshares developed. Fireworks used for festivals.

221 BCE–206 CE Qin dynasty. Construction begins on the Great Wall and on the tomb of the First Emperor at Lishan Mountain. Dragon kilns are built inside Lishan for the tomb ceramics. Weights, axle length, and calligraphy standardized.

206 BCE–220 CE Han dynasty. Batten sails, staggered masts, and watertight compartments used in shipbuilding. The harness and the stirrup used efficiently. Three-lane imperial highways built throughout the empire. Standardized iron tools made for agriculture. Zhang Heng invents the seismograph, as well as longitude and latitude for mapping.

second century BCE Rotary winnowing fan for processing grain improves production. The swan-neck hoe and the multi-tube seed drill are used for planting crops.

first century BCE The wheelbarrow is invented.

first century CE The endless chain water pump used for irrigation is created. Suspension bridges are developed.

second century Cai Lun invents paper.

seventh century Printing is invented.

ninth century Movable type made of clay is devised.

tenth century The flamethrower, using gunpowder, is developed for warfare.

1000 Magnetic needle compass for navigation is in wide use.

1368–1644 Ming dynasty.

1200s Europeans and Arabs adopt Chinese navigational compass. Gunpowder comes to the attention of the West.

1970s The tomb of Marchioness of Dai found with beautiful silks dating from 150 BCE.

1989 Dr. Qin Dahe, meteorologist, is the first Chinese person to reach the South Pole.

2006 Railway links Tibet to the heart of China.

2014 Three Gorges Dam is complete.

2015 Earthquake measuring 6.5 on Richter scale hits Xianjiang, China, kills four and injures many others. West Loop high-speed rail line opens on Hainan Island.

Glossary

alloy A mixture of two or more chemical elements, at least one of which is a metal. Bronze is an alloy made of tin and copper.

altitude The vertical distance of an object above a surface.

archaeologist A scientist who studies the physical remains of past human life and activities.

ballast Heavy material placed in a ship to ensure stability.

battens Long, flat strips of squared lumber used to hold something in place.

cheng Literally "wall," the word has come to mean "city" in China from the defensive walls surrounding ancient Chinese cities.

conscripted Taken into military or other service compulsively; drafted.

culture heroes Legendary figures who are credited with the bestowal of farming, hunting, fishing, and writing upon the ancient Chinese.

dialects Different varieties of speech within a single language peculiar to particular regions or groups.

dynasty A line of hereditary rulers. The Xia dynasty was China's first dynasty.

endless chain pump A turnover wheel powered by leg muscles that is used for raising water to irrigate elevated plots.

furrow The narrow trench made in the surface of the earth by a plow in preparation for planting.

geomancy Divination by means of geographical features. The Chinese used geomancy in the location and layout of cities and homes. The Chinese term is *feng shui,* literally "wind-water."

hopper A funnel-shaped box that is used to carry grain.

hull The underside of a ship.

kiln Furnace or oven used for firing clay objects in the process of pottery making.

lodestone A naturally magnetic iron oxide used in the first compasses.

loess A yellow, sandy silt that originates in the Gobi Desert and is blown by westerly winds across the plains of northern China.

longitude and latitude Imaginary lines drawn around the earth. Lines of longitude, or meridians, run from the North Pole to the South Pole.

Mandate of Heaven A Chinese philosophical and political concept in which the rule of the emperor is judged by Heaven to be either just or unjust. Heaven sends appropriate signs via natural disasters or blessings.

mausoleum A large burial chamber for the entombment of the dead. Lishan is the site of the First Emperor's mausoleum.

metallurgy The science and technology of metals.

millet A grass growing in Asia and Europe that is used for its grain.

pounded earth Ancient Chinese durable building technology in which loess is compacted by means of cobblestone pestles. Called *hang tu* in Chinese.

Richter scale A system for measuring the strength of earthquakes; ranging from 1 to 10.

saltpeter Potassium nitrate, a white crystalline substance used in making gunpowder and other items.

seismograph An instrument that measures and records the force and direction of vibrations in the earth such as earthquakes.

sericulture Silkworm breeding and all the stages in the production of silk.

Silk Road A series of trade routes that ran through northern China, connecting it with lands to the west.

superpower A country that has great influence, monetary strength, and political power.

terra-cotta Literally "baked earth." The fired clay used for statues and architectural purposes such as pipes and conduits. The terra-cotta warriors found at Lishan are examples of China's famous ceramics technology.

threshing Beating out or separating grain from the dried straw or stalks.

winnowing To blow grain free of chaff (seed husks and other debris).

Further Information

Books

Atkins, Marcie Flinchum. *Ancient China*. Ancient Civilizations. Edina, MN: Essential Library, 2015.

Collins, Terry. *Ancient China: An Interactive History Adventure*. You Choose: Historical Eras. North Mankato, MN: Capstone Press, 2012.

Friedman, Mel. *Ancient China*. True Books. New York: Scholastic, 2010.

Morley, Jacqueline. *You Wouldn't Want to Work on the Great Wall of China!* New York: Scholastic, 2006.

Osborne, Mary Pope, and Natalie Pope Boyce. *China: Land of the Emperor's Great Wall*. Magic Tree House Fact Tracker. New York: Random House, 2014.

Websites

Ducksters: Ancient China

http://www.ducksters.com/history/china/ancient_china.php

Learn about all sorts of topics about ancient China at this website.

History for Kids: Exploring Ancient China

http://www.historyforkids.net/ancient-china.html

Take a tour of ancient China at this website.

Index

Page numbers in **boldface** are illustrations. Entries in **boldface** are glossary terms.